SOLO GUITAR

CELTIC FAVORITES
FOR OPEN-TUNED GUITAR

Arranged by Jeff Jacobson

ISBN 1-57560-448-5

Visit our website at www.cherrylane.com

DANNY BOY
(LONDONDERRY AIR)

Traditional

Tuning:
(low to high) E–A–D–E–A–D

Moderately, with feeling

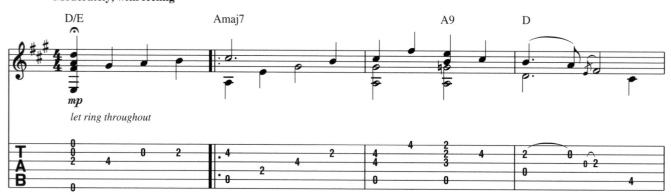

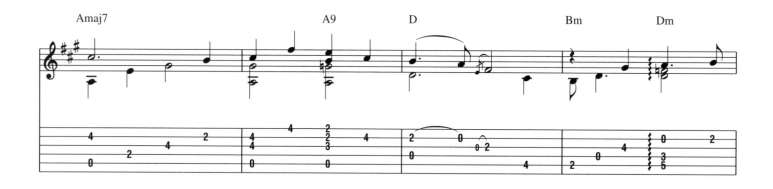

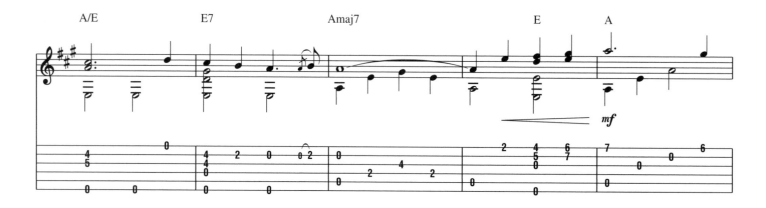

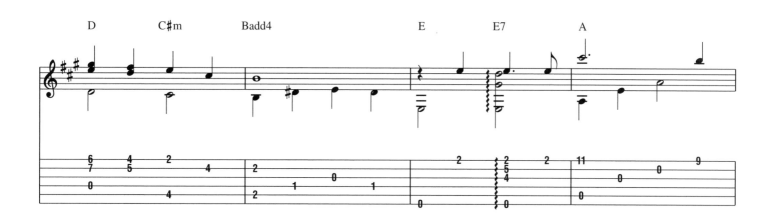

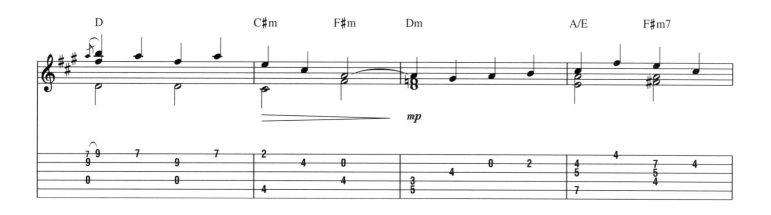

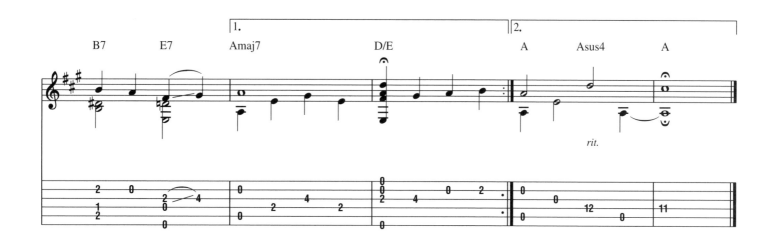

HAS SORROW THY YOUNG DAYS SHADED?

Traditional

Tuning:
(low to high) D–A–D–E–A–D

Moderately slow

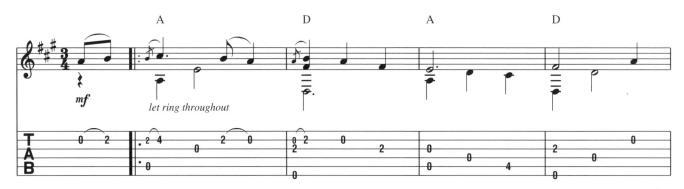

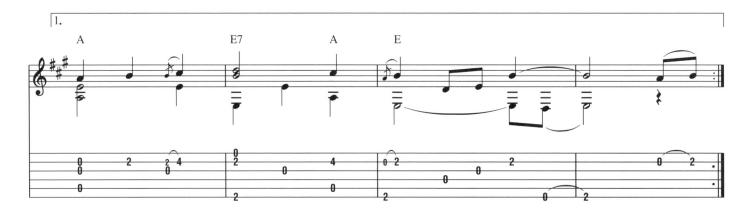

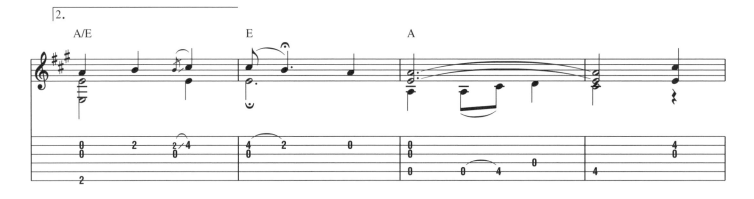

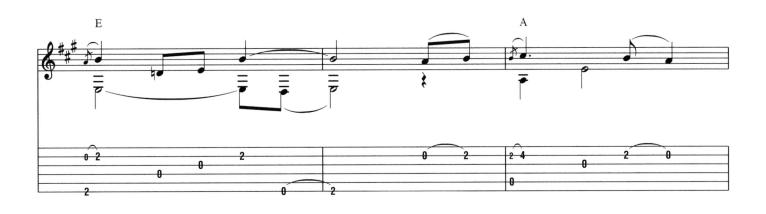

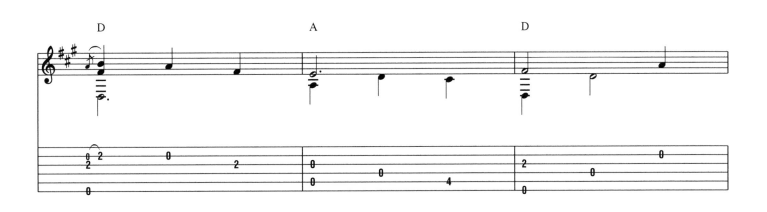

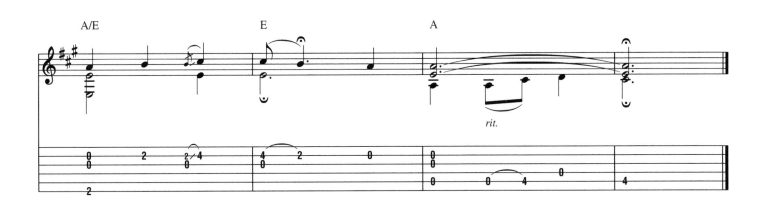

HASTE TO THE WEDDING

Traditional

Tuning:
(low to high) D–A–D–G–A–D

Moderately

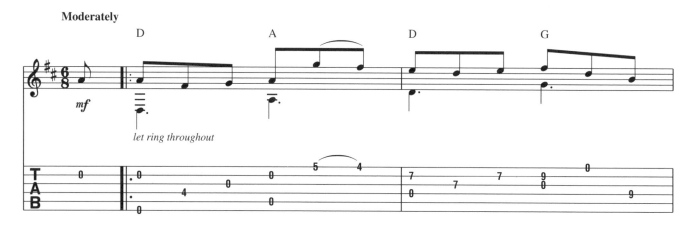

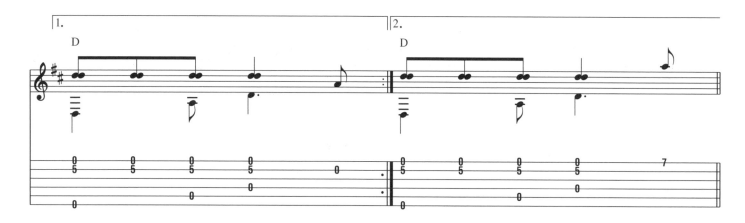

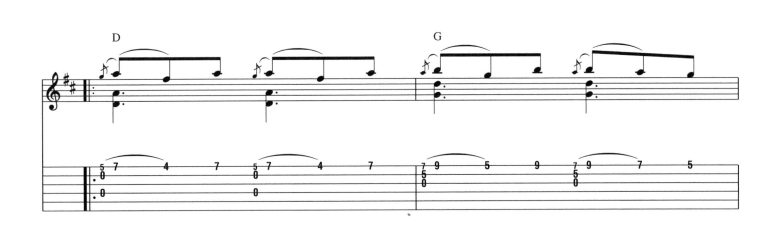

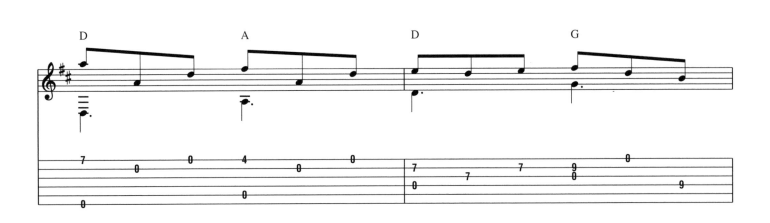

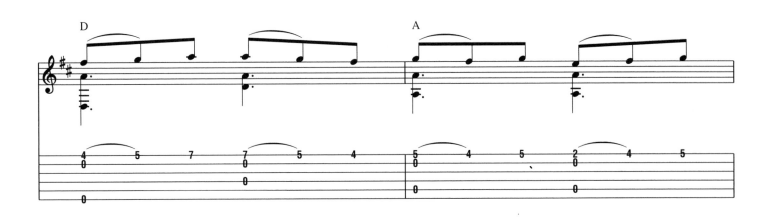

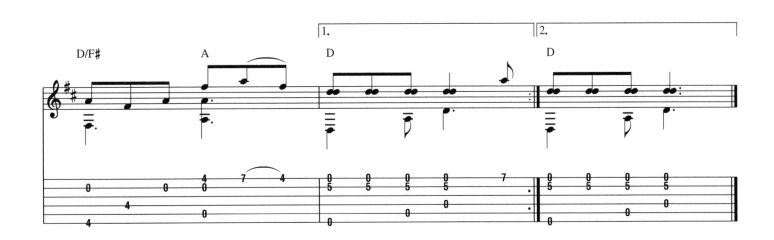

CORNISH MAY DANCE

Traditional

Drop D tuning:
(low to high) D–A–D–G–B–E

HOLE IN THE WALL

Traditional

Tuning:
(low to high) E–A–D–F♯–A–E

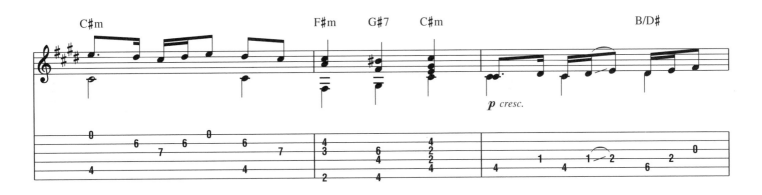

11

KATHLEEN MAVOUREEN

Traditional

Tuning:
(low to high) D–A–D–G–A–E

Moderately

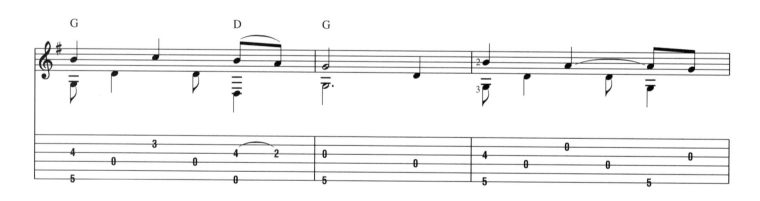

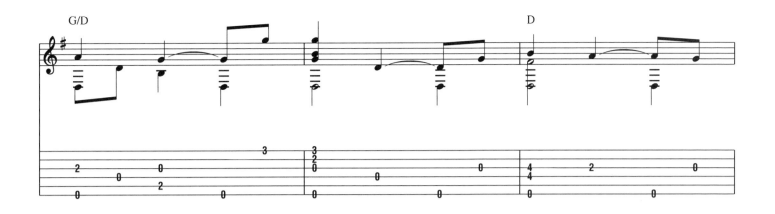

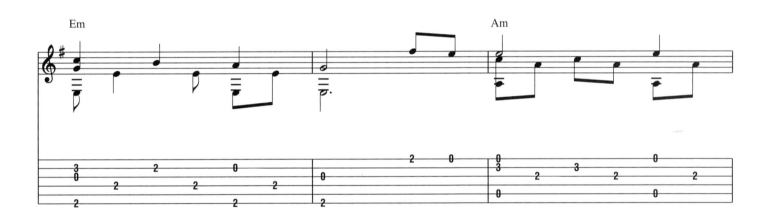

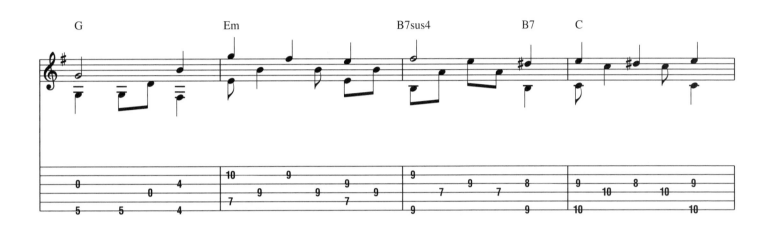

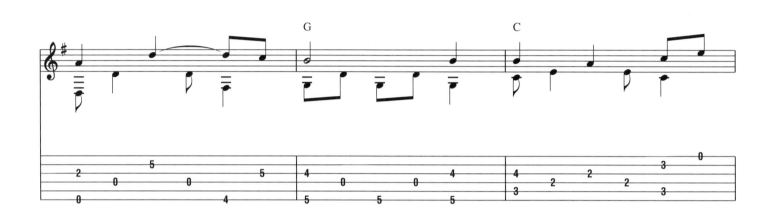

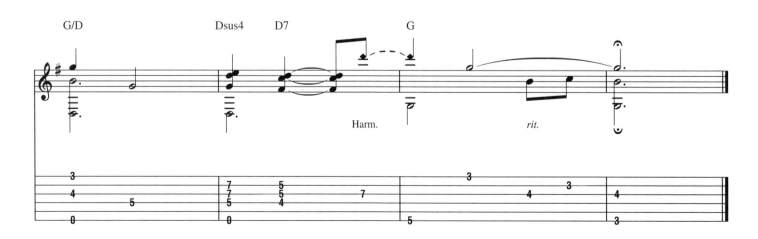

THE MINSTREL BOY

Traditional

Tuning:
(low to high) D–A–D–G–A–D

Moderately

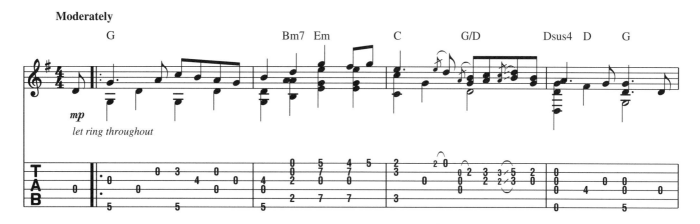

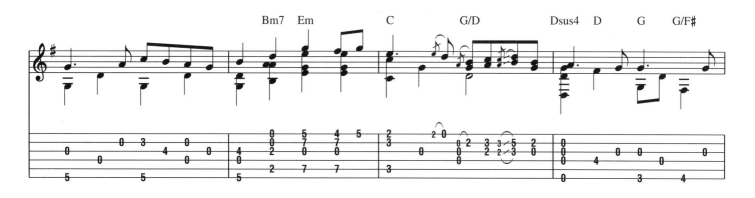

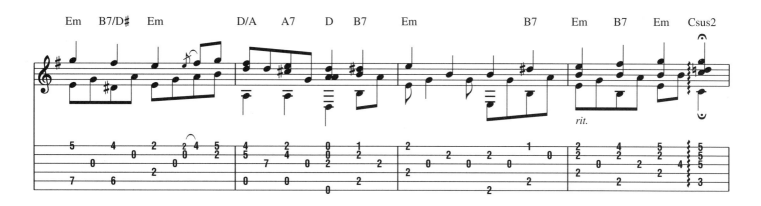

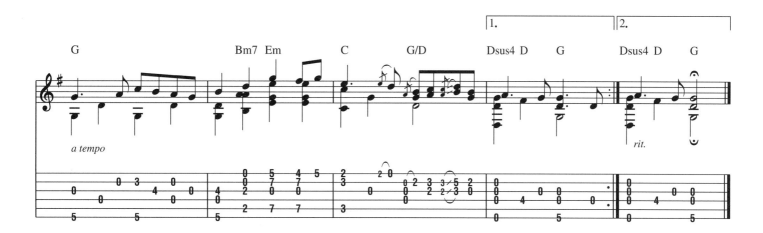

KERRY DANCE

By J.L. Molloy

Tuning:
(low to high) E–A–D–E–A–D

Brightly

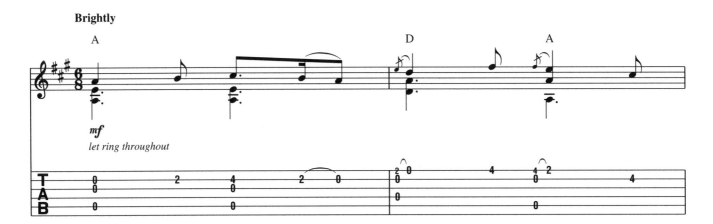

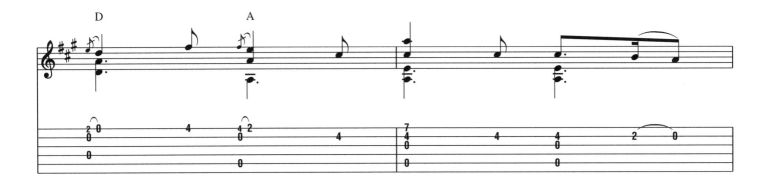

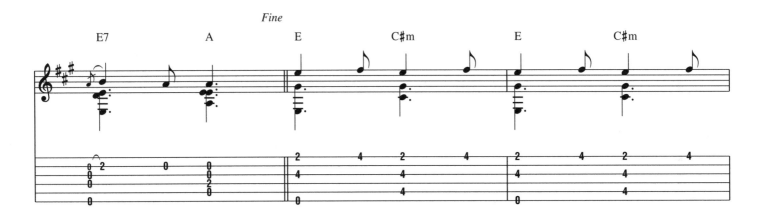

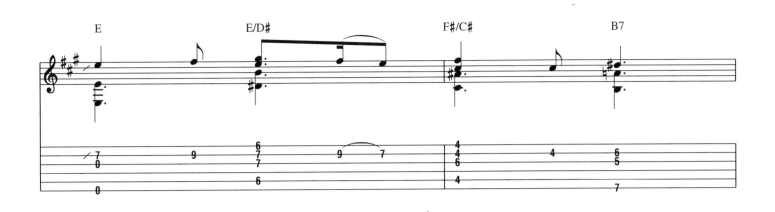

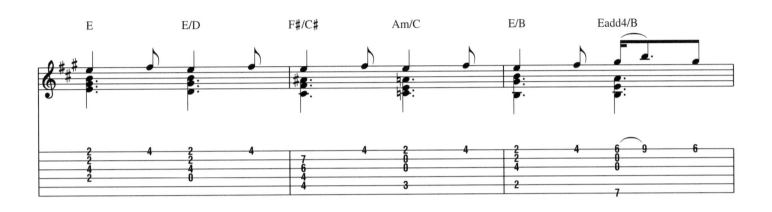

D.C. al Fine

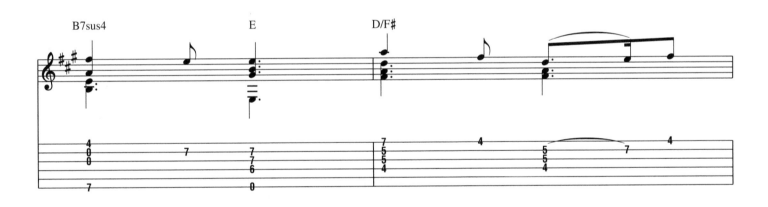

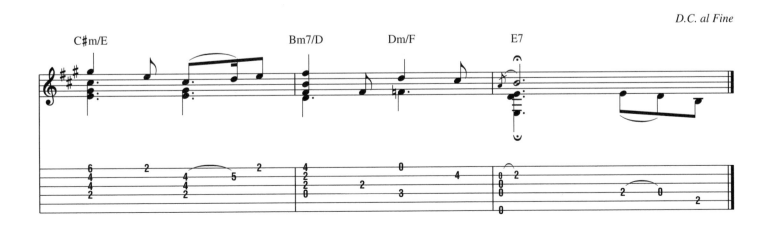

KILLARNEY

Traditional

Tuning:
(low to high) E–A–D–E–A–E

Moderately

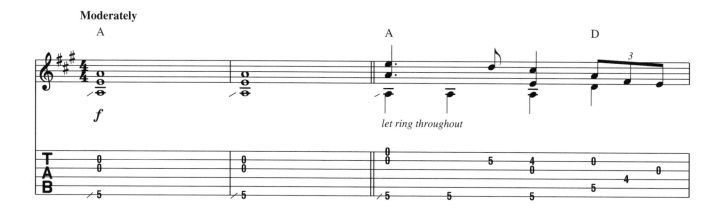

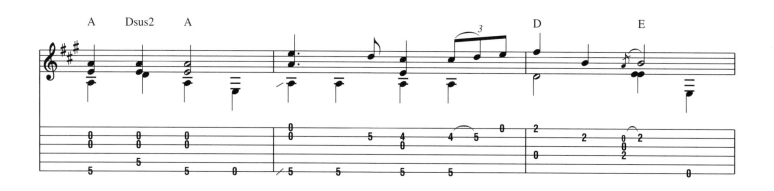

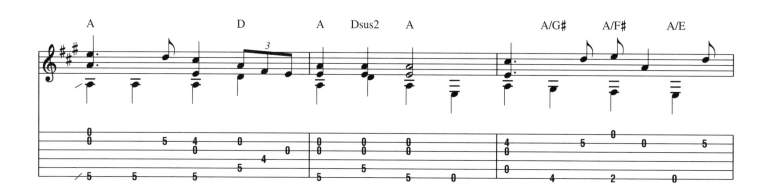

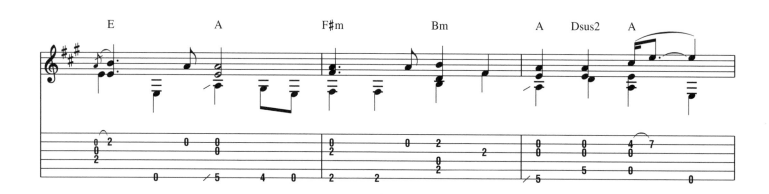

MOLLY MALONE
(COCKLES & MUSSELS)

Traditional

Tuning:
(low to high) E–A–D–E–A–E

Moderately slow

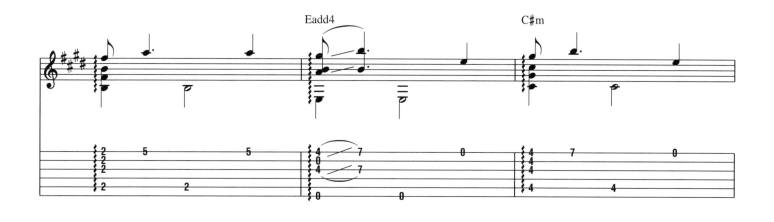

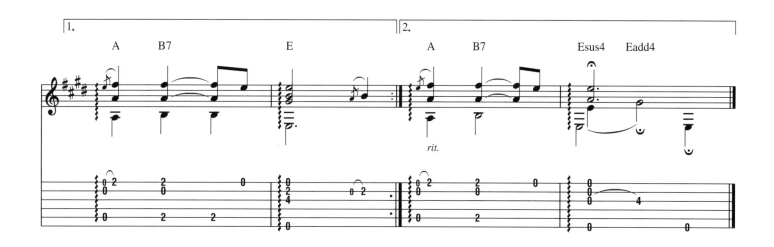

MOTHER MACHREE

Traditional

Tuning:
(low to high) D–A–D–G–A–D

Moderately, with feeling

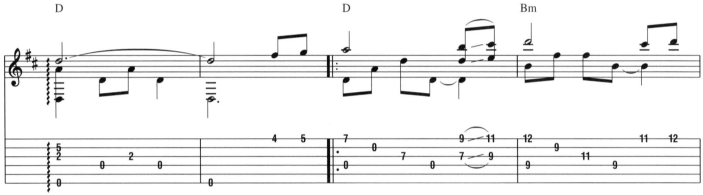

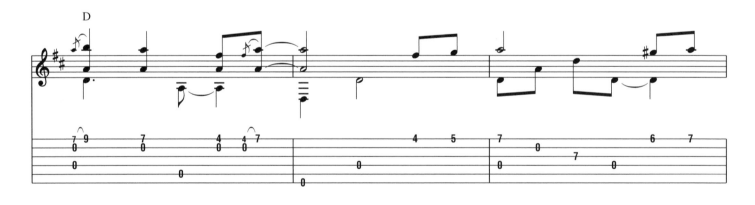

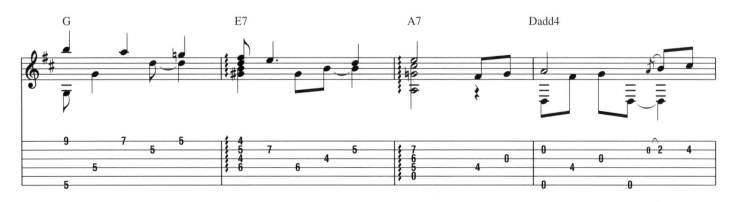

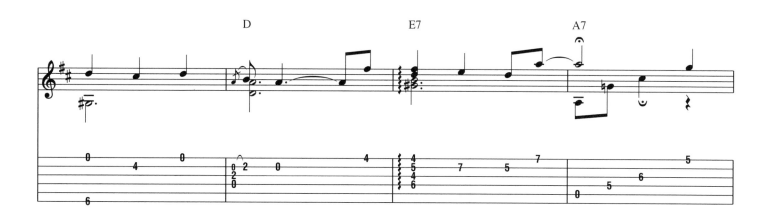

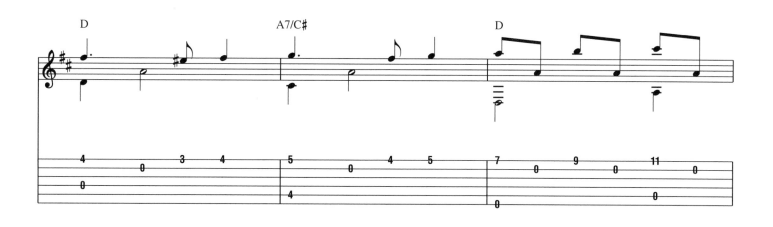

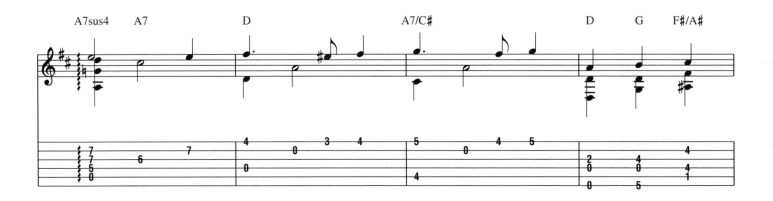

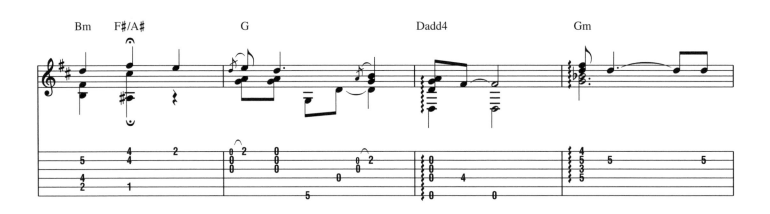

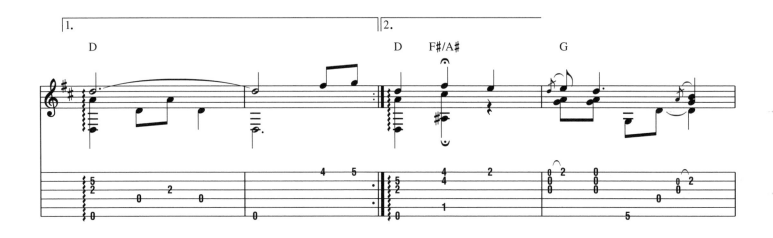

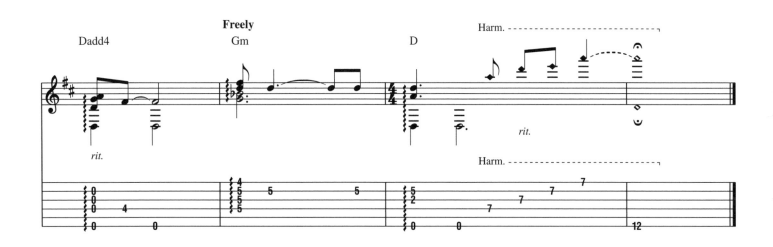

THE SKYE BOAT SONG

Traditional

Tuning:
(low to high) D–A–D–E–A–D

Moderately

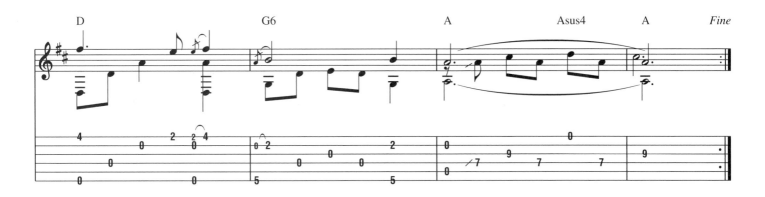

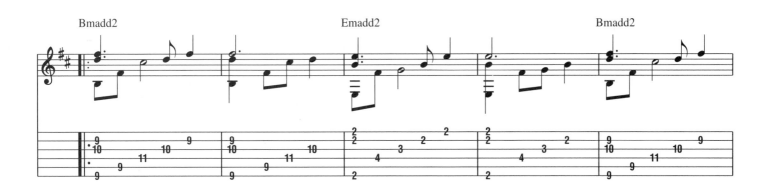

ROSIN THE BOW

Traditional

Tuning:
(low to high) D–A–D–G–A–D

Moderately fast

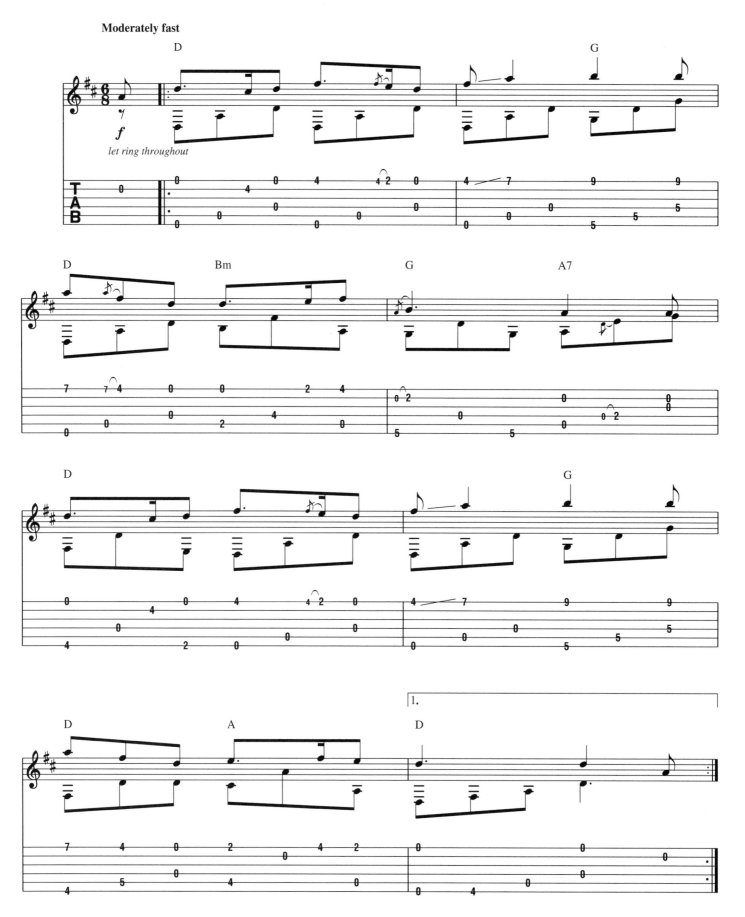

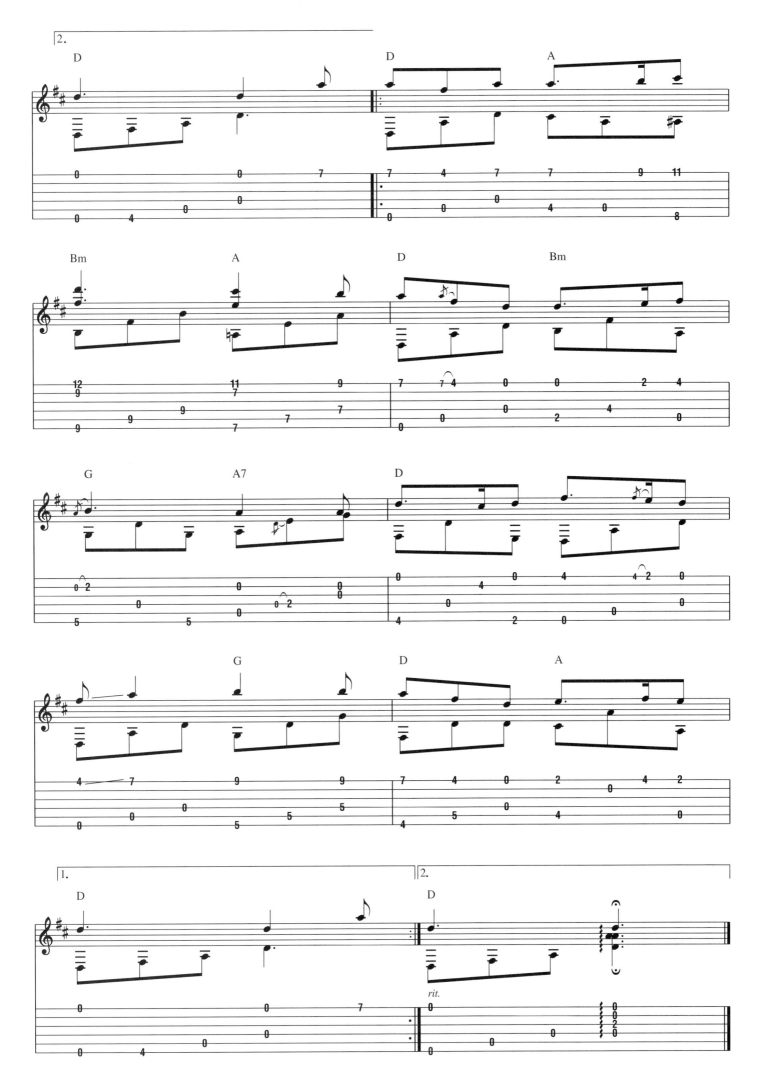

'TIS THE LAST ROSE OF SUMMER

Traditional

Tuning:
(low to high) E–A–D–E–A–D

Slowly and tenderly

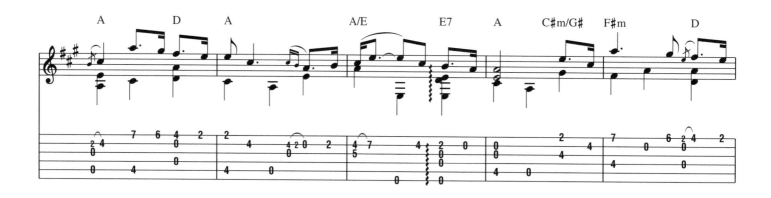

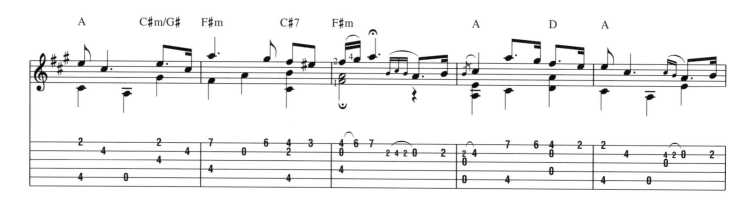

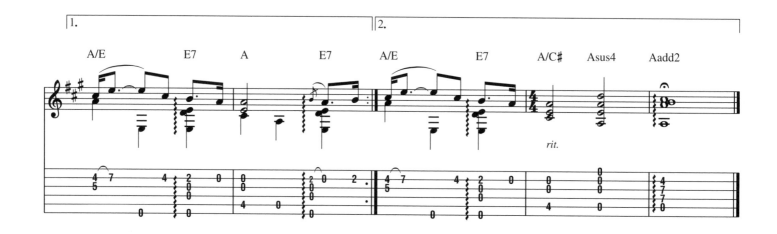

THE WATER IS WIDE

Traditional

Tuning:
(low to high) D–A–D–G–A–D

Moderately

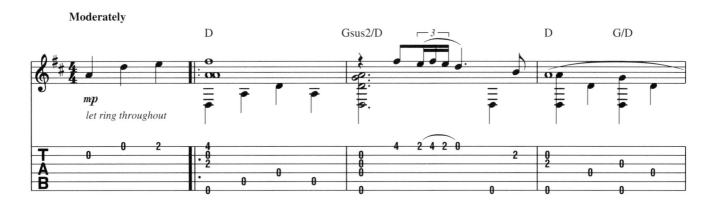

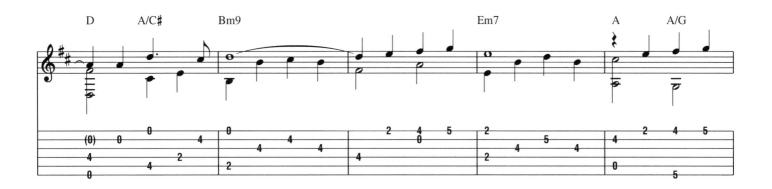

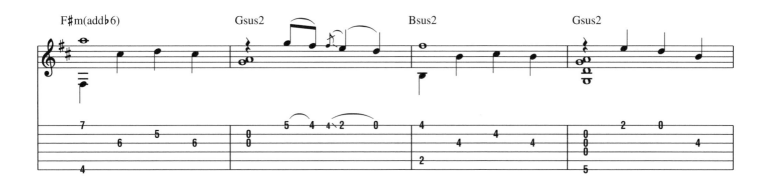

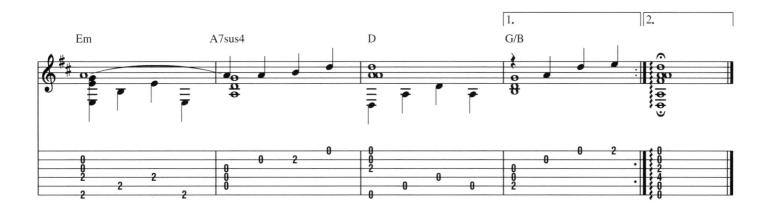

29

WHERE THE RIVER SHANNON FLOWS

Traditional

Tuning:
(low to high) D–A–D–G–A–E

Moderately, with feeling

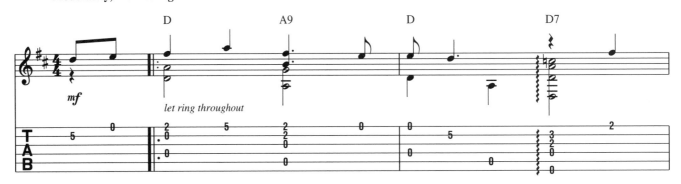

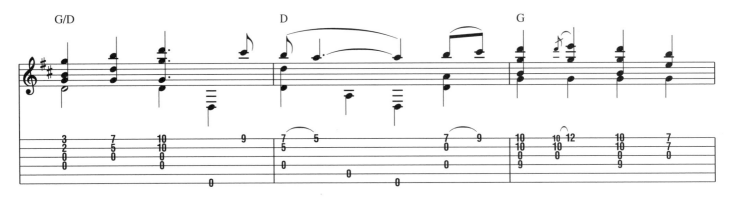